Soaring with Eagles...
Hangin' with Buzzards

Soaring with Eagles… Hangin' with Buzzards

(How Your Attitude Determines Your Altitude)

By

Pastor Anthony Sluzas

Soaring with Eagles ... Hangin' with Buzzards

Copyright © 2008 by Pastor Anthony Sluzas

All rights reserved. No part of this book may be reproduced, stored, or transmitted by any means—whether auditory, graphic, mechanical, or electronic—without written permission of both publisher and author, except in the case of brief excerpts used in critical articles and reviews. Unauthorized reproduction of any part of this work is illegal and is punishable by law.

ISBN: **To be determined.**

Library of Congress Control Number: **To be determined.**

Contents

Acknowledgements	vii
Introduction	1
Fly Like An Eagle	5
"Wah Wah" (Excuses: We've Got A Million)	11
You Can't Hide Those Lying Eyes	17
Slip-Sliding Away	23
I Resent That!	29
It's My Life	33
Child, You Mind Your Daddy!	41
Meathead	47
All of Me	53

This book is dedicated to a true man of God who I consider to be my mentor and friend, Pastor Stan Tharp.

Acknowledgements

I want to acknowledge and thank all of you who never gave up on me during my B.C. years, though I'd given you every reason to do exactly that. I thank most of all, the Lord Jesus Christ, who lovingly and mercifully reached down, and pulled me out of a cesspool of degradation, and saved my soul more than twenty years ago. I am also indebted more than she'll ever realize; to my wife, Debbie, and my 'babies,' Katie and Jacob, who are growing up much too quickly. My family means everything to me and I'd be lost without them. I want to thank my mother, Elinor Sluzas, and sister, Annamarie Berger for loving me unconditionally, and for showing me what it really means to be a Christian. And finally, many thanks go to people like my best friend in ministry, and on this planet; Pastor Randy McKinney, as well as a heaven-sent, 'guardian angel,' Lauren Taylor, and to Sally at Harmony Farm in Tipp City, Ohio. Jane Kronenberger, you don't know how much you have blessed my life when my flame was barely a flicker. Thank you, for your help and encouragement, Evangelist Tim Enloe, Myra Swartz, and a good many others who have been urging me to "write some sort of book;" by whom it's my privilege and honor to be called "Pastor" at Fresh Harvest Church in Morgantown, West Virginia for the past six years. I hope you're blessed by this, my first attempt at writing a manuscript. Thank you all.

May the Lord bless and keep you.

Introduction

The book you are holding in your hand is not a study in wildlife. It is, however, about *eagles.* It is also about *buzzards.* Most importantly, it's about *you.* First off, I want to make it crystal clear that I am not a zookeeper; nor am I an expert on birds of prey. I did have a parakeet once when I was seven. No, I'm just a regular guy; a husband, father, and pastor. My heart's desire is to *find a need, and meet that need.* (That is the simplest and most to-the-point definition of the word "ministry" I've ever heard. I cannot take credit for this definition. It came straight from Jesus Christ, in the pages of the Bible.) I am writing to you today, because in my small way, I want to be of help to you, and in so doing, yield myself to God for His glory.

Dear friend, I want to start off by asking a couple of personal questions: **I am asking, right now, wherever you are, with God's help, to begin taking a brutally honest look inward;** *taking a personal inventory, if you will, of your spiritual, attitudinal, emotional, and relational health and wellbeing.* As you take a long, hard look at the sum total of your life up to this point in time; *are you soaring with eagles, or hangin' with buzzards?*

I can almost hear some of you now…

"Say what? What do eagles and buzzards have to do with me? Tony, what in heaven's name are you talking about?"

Please allow me to begin the process of painting a vivid portrait upon the canvas of your mind, even as, I believe, God wants to speak to your heart today.

In your mind's eye; picture a mighty eagle soaring majestically through bright blue skies.

We all know that the eagle is a popular mascot to countless elementary, high school, college, and professional sports teams. The American Bald Eagle is our nation's symbol. Most of us are fascinated by the eagle. You'd be hard pressed to find another creature on the planet as regal or majestic. Appearing to fly almost effortlessly, with great power being released from its muscular body and massive wingspan, the eagle soars through the open skies as it commands the awe and respect of all who behold him. Then, suddenly, almost as if turning on the "after-burners," he rockets upward, leaving the world far behind, soaring to unbelievable heights. Whenever I've witnessed that amazing spectacle, I'll just quote the late, great Cubs announcer, Harry Caray, by shouting aloud, "Holy cow!"

What is it that captures our imagination, enthralls, and draws our attention to this magnificent creature? Obviously, there are many, and varied responses to this question. However, I believe that first and foremost, we can and should to go to the "Creator's Handbook" to find absolute truth, and get His perspective. Yes it's true; because even in the pages of the Bible, you can read about the majestic eagle. Years ago, when I began searching the Bible for answers to the mess that was my life, I "stumbled upon" some of these specific passages.

I have always been enamored with the American bald eagle in particular, but while reading about the eagle in God's Word, I was floored; blown-away upon discovering how God, the Creator of the entire universe, draws specific and detailed analogies between Himself and all of us--to the eagle. It was, in a word-amazing. Again, please indulge my excitement; "Holy cow!"

Conversely, at the opposite end of the spectrum; I give you, **the buzzard.**

All in all, the buzzard is a rather loathsome creature which repels, rather than, attracting onlookers. The buzzard induces fear and dread to the already dying. It is nature's symbol of death and destruction.

After digging deeply into Scripture, and having been blessed to sit under great teachers, as well as studying other wonderful books, and periodicals on the subject, I began to see that there was something very unique and special about the eagle; so much so, that God would want His children to gain spiritual and practical insight into *His nature*, and *ours*. What you are reading right now, was actually a series of weekend messages that I delivered to our congregation at Fresh Harvest Church in Morgantown, West Virginia. I have expanded the content of my material in order to benefit you, the reader. Over the last six years, a number of people, including my wife, Debbie, have encouraged and urged me to write a book(s). I do believe that God used these dear people to give me, a sometimes, not-so-gentle nudge from out of the nest. So now, having just turned 50, I'd finally decided the time had come to begin writing my first in a series of manuscripts, God willing.

And here I sit, in a local Starbucks with my Bible, HP notebook, and a 'triple venti latte,' across the street from West Virginia University, hunting and pecking away on this, my first manuscript. My prayer for you, dear friend, is that the Spirit of the living God will "open the eyes of your heart," that you will begin to see how much He loves and cares *for you*. The Holy Spirit will teach you how to live a truly victorious life here and now, in preparation for a glorious eternity with God.

1

Fly Like An Eagle

"Like an eagle that stirs up its nest; that hovers over its young, He spread His wings and caught them. He carried them on His pinions" (Deuteronomy 32:11, NKJV).

Upon emerging from the warmth and security of its egg, after pecking and struggling to break free; a fuzzy, awkward little eaglet enters the world. Its Mama makes sure his every need is met. The little guy will sit there in the soft, feathery, cushy nest just chillin.' Everything he needs in life to sustain him is brought "special delivery" by his protective parent. Life is great! After a while, however, things gradually begin to change as this little guy is now growing, little by little, beyond infancy. Something is different, and the little eaglet isn't quite sure he likes the changes that are happening around him. It now seems, whatever the reason, Mama is stirring up the nest. What is she doing? She has begun to get restless it seems, and is now flapping her wings as she moves around the nest. What's up? Is she cleaning house today? It's not Saturday already, is it? Wait a minute: Mama's starting to take away all those soft comfy feathers and leaves that were lining the nest. Hey, what's happening to the crib? Now when little dude tries to lie down, the nest is prickly, and poking at him. Hey, things aren't as comfy as they used to be! Why is Mama doing this? What's happening?

The time has come in the life of the eaglet to grow up.

You may be able to somehow identify with this little guy right about now. Your Heavenly Father has provided for you; He's nourished, and nurtured you every step of the way. However, you may have even been walking with God for a quite a while now, but you're not feeling as comfortable or as enthusiastic as you once were. Things you once passionately believed are turning stale. You even may be fighting a losing battle against doubt. What was once a "river of life" flowing through your entire being, has instead become stifled, and stagnant through the monotony of lifeless ritual, and mere human traditions.

You now suffer from a type of "constipation of creativity" because your wildly imaginative and creative ideas have been shot down one too many times at the office, the PTO, or possibly, even at your church. You may have contemplated just throwing in the towel and giving up.

Sometimes people reach a point in life where they wonder why things aren't as comfy and cozy as they used to be. Dear one, that's called *"change."* People cringe when they hear *that word,* but change is an integral part of life. God has created all living organisms for *change,* and *growth.* Either they will go with the flow of God's design for change and maturation; *or they will die.* God may be stirring up your little (spiritual, physical, relational, emotional, or financial) nest just as the adult eagle stirs up its nest and forces its little ones to "Get up, and get ready to fly!" All that stuff you've trusted in for so long doesn't seem so secure anymore. God is trying to help you to get up, and begin to move from beyond your little comfort zone in order to *change you* and *mature you.* Father God wants you to genuinely *trust* in Him. He wants you to *serve* Him. He wants you to *serve others.* Just like with that precious little eaglet: It may be time for you to grow up. Please stop moping and complaining about the upheaval that change inevitably brings into your life. Break the cycle of running away to "greener pastures" when things get hard. God may very well be whispering to you at this moment, *"Little one, it's time to begin growing up now."*

Experts say that after several days of the adult eagle stirring up the nest, and making her eaglets move around their now; prickly and uncomfortable home, that Mama begins to position herself behind them. I think you know what happens next…She flutters her great wings and pushes the eaglet up, and on to the very edge of the nest, when all of a sudden, *"Uh-oh,"* down he goes! By sheer instinct, he starts desperately flailing and flapping his puny wings just like he's seen Mama and Papa do, but it's futile. Downward he goes…faster and faster.

Then, at the last possible moment, the little one's Mama shoots down from on high after him, and then underneath him; now gently carrying the eaglet on her wings, and back to their nest.

Are you looking over into a massive chasm? Looking down upon a situation seemingly impossible to overcome? You may feel as if you're in "freefall" and frantically flapping your "faith wings." It may appear that you're about to hit rock-bottom with a "splat!" But dear friend, I'm telling you that *your heavenly Father will not let you fall.*

Long, long ago, after delivering the Israelites from Egyptian bondage, God said to His chosen people, **"You have seen what I did to the Egyptians, and how I bore you on eagles wings, and brought you to Myself" (Exodus 19:4, NKJV).**

After spending the night in the safety and security of the nest; this little bird isn't out of the woods yet because the very next day, they'll go through the same exercise all over again! However, this time around, he's stronger, he knows what's coming, and he actually flies just a little before he is again rescued by his parent.

Several days later, after more testing and repetition of this exercise: *He does it!* This little one begins soaring with wings outstretched. *"Hey, hey, look at me. This is so cool!"*

Just like the eagle, it takes time to strengthen your spiritual wings, but keep on, constantly exercising them. God plainly shows you when it's time to *spread your wings* and learn how to soar, by faith in Him and His Word, above the tests, trials, and impossibilities of your life-to victory.

Sadly, too many people simply will not hear from God; *until they take a risk(s).* You're going to have to make yourself step out of your nest of spiritual infancy, and complacency, and learn to trust God. Don't be afraid to *"flap those wings of faith."* God has made you to soar, and you will--*if* you will just begin: Move, be bold, and do something!

Nothing is impossible with God. He has so much good in store for you. When you soar in faith; there are no limits with the Lord. You and I are the only ones who can limit the power of God in our lives.

Just how big, and how outrageous can *you* dream for God? Your answer to this question will determine your spiritual altitude or how high you will soar in life with Christ.

Look at God's Word, and you'll discover that the Lord will never put limits on your faith. See what Jesus has to say:

"...and nothing shall be impossible to you" (Matthew 17:20, NKJV).

"...whatever things you ask when you pray, believe that you receive them, and you will have them" (Mark 11:24, NJKV).

The apostle Paul being led by the Holy Spirit; wrote the following:

"I can do all things through Christ, who strengthens me" (Philippians 4:13, NKJV).

How high will you soar in life with God? Remember now: No limits! Learn from the eagle, loved one: Build your "nest" on the sure foundation-on God's Word-and build it strong so that it'll stand the tests and trials of this life. Next, test your spiritual wings by faith! This is something *only you* can do for yourself. Your Dad, your Mom, sister, brother, spouse, or even your Pastor can't live by faith for you. God, Himself, can't do it for you. *It's up to you.*

Will you believe God, and take Him at His Word? If you will, He will fill you with His Spirit of faith, and in time, you'll be soaring over the chasm of impossibilities with the word of faith as your fuel and your strength. Dare to believe God for great things! Dare to dream big, outrageous, God-sized dreams!

Take an honest, spiritual inventory, and find out where your faith level is; then decide exactly what you can believe God for right now.

Next, put your faith to work. Exercise it, and then receive the answers to those things that you believe God for. Your faith will be strengthened and will grow to maturity. Keep in mind that the eagle doesn't have great power in its wings to begin with: His wings must be developed.

Perhaps you're just feeling beaten down by life and thoroughly discouraged today. Maybe you are thinking to yourself at this moment; "I sure don't feel like I can fly on eagles' wings. I feel more like an old buzzard. I am about as low as a person can get." Your loving heavenly Father is speaking to you today, loved one:

"Do you not know? Have you not heard?

The Everlasting God, the Lord, the Creator of the ends of the earth,

(He) does not become weary or tired. His understanding is inscrutable.

He gives strength to the weary, and to him who lacks might, He increases power.

Though youths grow weary and tired, and vigorous young men stumble badly,

Yet those who wait for the Lord will gain new strength;

They will mount up with wings like eagles

They will run and not get tired,

They will walk and not become weary"
(Isaiah 40:28-31).

We need to keep on stretching ourselves spiritually, and exercising our wings of faith. How does a believer do that? You and I can build and strengthen our faith by diligently feeding on, and then doing God's Word, and by living a life of worship, thanksgiving and praise.

It's time to fly! It doesn't matter if you're standing with your knees-knocking on the edge of your safe and comfy nest for the first time or if you've been soaring with the Lord for years. Our God will not let you fall and He will never fail you.

The purpose of this book is to show you that it is *possible* to not only dream the impossible dream, but also to achieve the seemingly impossible, through faith in Jesus Christ.

Does your attitude resemble that of an eagle, or a buzzard? It's a very important question for you to consider, *because your attitude will determine your altitude!*

2

"Wah Wah"
(Excuses: We've Got A Million)

"But he who endures to the end shall be saved"
(Mark 13:13b, NKJV).

People make hundreds of excuses as to why they're living in defeat these days. There is a serious "victim mentality" and "self-centeredness" that's infecting our society, and is now pervasive--even in the Church of Jesus Christ. Sadly, too many of God's people are experts at making excuses for producing scrawny crops. The real issue here is quite simply, *unbelief,* and a *lousy* attitude. There are folks in many walks of life, and working in a vast array of professions who achieve little to no success because:

"Things are really hard all over."

"I can't accept that job offer because it's too far for me to drive, and gasoline's too expensive."

"Why do I get all of the grumpy and cheap customers? My tips are awful!"

"There must be a recession."

"People are only looking. They're not going to buy."
"This job sucks."
"It's too hot to work."
"It's too cold."
"If it weren't for bad luck, I'd have no luck at all."

Loved one, ***you will reap what you sow!*** Whatever you ***plant*** in the spiritual realm, in the emotional/relational realm, in the physical realm, and in the financial realm; ***will grow, multiply, and come back to you***-thirty, sixty, and one hundred-fold! It's a spiritual law set forth by Jesus Christ.

Some of you may be talking back to your book right about now and saying, "Wait a minute, Tony. My workplace is a controlled environment. I just can't change things there on my own." Oh yes, you certainly can. You can perform your job better than anyone else in your office, and those people with clout will eventually take notice. Pursue excellence and God will reward you. Feed your faith and be positively positive. Show enthusiasm, and your surroundings will change!

I don't know about you but I want to walk by faith. I want to be a loving, compassionate, positive and upbeat person. I do not want to drag others down by my being negative; full of doubt and unbelief. It must be clearly understood that fear activates Satan's power just as faith activates the power of God.

Faith and unbelief are diametrically opposing forces:

Faith always has a dream much larger than oneself.

Unbelief sees only the sad state where I'm now stuck in spiritual quicksand.

Faith says, "Here, let me give you a hand."

Unbelief says, "It's not my job, man."

Faith says, "I live to give. In fact, I can't afford not to tithe. I enjoy sowing into the church and other peoples' lives."

Unbelief says, "I can't afford to tithe. That's Old Testament anyway; dead and gone. It doesn't apply to us now." (That's ignorance gone to seed. Read your New Testament. It's taught multiple times, and reinforced by Jesus, Himself.)

Faith says, "The odds are against us. It's never been done before but I believe it's possible."

Unbelief says, "This is too risky. It can't be done. It's impossible."

We need to heed the words of the Savior, **"By their fruits you will know them" (Matthew 7:20, NKJV).** Those who bear much fruit truly understand God's principle of sowing and reaping. If you as an individual, and the Church as a whole, desire to prepare our field(s) for a fresh harvest, we must focus on our opportunities instead of the obstacles. If you want to reap a great harvest, you must put some seed into the ground! If you desire a great harvest in your life and career, it will not come as a result of your amazing GPA, or by dumb luck, or because of a 'phat' inheritance from a rich relative. This huge harvest comes to those who sow seed generously and liberally, consistently tilling the ground, and who never ever quits, who reaps a record crop!

An essential item that enriches soil is fertilizer. Fertilizer is a lot like a person's attitude: When fertilizer is spread around; generously worked and with care, it will then facilitate the growth of a most impressive and abundant crop. However, if you carelessly just leave that same fertilizer lying out in a giant heap and not put it to work by refusing to spread it around your field, it will only yield one big stink! *Attitude* is probably the least expensive possession that you own, but you need to realize it will produce some of the greatest crops you've ever seen, or the biggest stink imaginable!

Ever had really bad service at a restaurant? You said, "Yes"?

Did you go back? Chances are, you didn't. Sure, you may have given them another shot but I dare say most people would not return to that restaurant. Market surveys have stated that one customer who's had a bad experience at an eatery, will tell seven other people about it, who in turn, tell seven more, and they tell seven more...on and on it goes! The opposite is also true. The individual who interacts with a friendly, upbeat, positive, and professional staff at a particular dining establishment, and enjoys delicious and well prepared food, will relay their wonderful experience to seven other folks, who each in turn, tell seven more, etc.

It all comes down to *attitude*, and your attitude determines your altitude. Will you soar victoriously on wings of *eagles* with your heavenly Father? Or would you rather slink around, and wallow in negativity, doubt, unbelief, and self pity with the *buzzards (Satan's domain)?*

Dear friend, you are a tri-partite being. Your entire being consists of three parts. You are a spirit. You don't have a spirit; you are a *spirit.* You have a *soul* consisting of your thoughts, free will and emotions. And for this short time on earth, you live inside a physical *body.* Our spirits are a lot like little sponges. We can soak in whatever we entertain and allow in through our five physical senses. Be very careful and watch what you feed your spirit with on a daily basis, because whatever is inside you will come out of your mouth when you're squeezed, and the pressure is on.

The choice is entirely up to you as to how you conduct yourself, and you will determine the atmosphere of your surroundings, and your future.

"Put away from you a deceitful mouth, and perverse lips far from you" (Proverbs 4:24, NKJV).

"Blessings are on the head of the righteous, but violence covers the mouth of the wicked" (Proverbs 10:6, NKJV).

"A soft answer turns away wrath, but a harsh word stirs up anger" (Proverbs 15:1, NKJV).

The workplace can be either incredibly fulfilling or it can be dreadfully negative and dark. Whatever you believe in your heart and then speak with your mouth, for good or bad, you will perpetuate. That's a spiritual principle found throughout the entirety of the Bible, and whether you personally believe that the Bible is the Word of God or not, *you are living by this principle!*

"Death and life are in the power of the tongue, and those who love it will eat its fruit" (Proverbs 18:21, NKJV).

What should you do when unbelieving or negative people bombard you with pessimism and gloom? How might you react to those who sow seeds of discord and strife? Do the Godly thing. Take the time and opportunity to bless them in some small way with the love of God. Accept the challenge of turning their frowns around into smiles! Realize who *you* are in Jesus Christ. Stand firmly on His Word and in His love!

If you truly are a follower of Jesus Christ, you should not be easily discouraged or offended, but consistently walk in love and forgiveness. Planting the seeds of love and compassion everywhere you go is an act of faith. You cultivate and water. You believe you will reap what you've sown, and even more! Keep on keeping on, believing, praying and saying, *"I can see my harvest is coming. I can see through the eyes of faith that my unbelieving family members are becoming believers. I believe I receive a miracle of healing for my fractured marriage. Lord, I believe that even now, you are healing my broken heart. I truly believe that God will use me to love the unlovely in my workplace and turn the entire situation around for good and for His glory!"*

(Jesus said,) "A good man out of the good treasure of his heart brings forth good; and an evil man out of the evil treasure of his heart brings forth evil. <u>For out of the abundance of his heart his mouth speaks</u>" (Luke 6:45, NKJV).

When the pressure is on people can tell by your words exactly what's inside you in abundance, and what you continually dwell on and speak aloud, you will bring to fruition and perpetuate in your life. *You are, right now,* the *sum total* of what you've believed in your heart, and every word you've ever spoken.

3

You Can't Hide Those Lying Eyes
("The father of lies" & temptation)

"He (Satan) was a murderer from the beginning, and does not stand in the truth, because there is no truth in him. When he speaks a lie, he speaks from his own resources, for he is a liar and the father of it" (John 8:44b).

A sure sign that an individual has been forgiven of his or her sins and is now a child of God; is the desire to avoid sin. Now that the sins of the past have been washed away, the born again believer is eager to pray, *"And lead us not into temptation, but deliver us from the evil one."*

I must begin this chapter by stating unequivocally that God does not lead His children into temptation. The literal translation of the Lord's Prayer into modern English of Matthew 6:13 in the TEV says, **"Do not bring us to hard testing, but keep us safe from the evil one,"** Please understand that God *does* allow us to be tested. The Bible says, *"God tested Abraham" (Genesis 22:1).* Of equal importance is the fact that God is *not* the one doing the tempting! **"Let no man say when he is**

tempted, 'I am tempted of God,' for God cannot be tempted with evil, neither does He tempt any man" (James 1:13).

Testing is meant for our good. It's not to harm us. A good school teacher who gives her students a test does not do it for the express purpose of sadistically failing young people in the class, even though it's given with the knowledge that some may fail. God didn't test Abraham to deliver him to Satan, but with the purpose that Abraham's faith in God's promise might prove strong and steadfast.

There are no great testimonies without our first conquering, and passing great tests. Character cannot be developed without tests. At Fresh Harvest we have some very gifted singers and musicians who lead us in worship every weekend. Our musicians, in particular, have not become as proficient as they are by continuing to play only the songs they'd learned when they were five years of age, such as, "Chopsticks." No way. Their musical skills were developed by stretching themselves beyond their comfort zones by repeatedly playing more difficult pieces. Again, dear friend, there's no testimony without a test...no victory without trials...no heroes without battling through great adversity and personal risk.

As long as you and I are alive on this earth we will contend daily with temptations of every kind. Our spiritual walk is a lot like what bodybuilders experience on a daily basis. These well trained, hard working physical specimens with sculpted and chiseled muscles go through an almost torturous daily regimen of pumping hundreds of pounds worth of iron and cardiovascular exercise just to be considered for a spot in a bodybuilding competition. These men and women must put themselves through the grind of repeatedly pushing and straining against heavy resistance in order to build up and strengthen their muscles. The Christian walk is very similar; in that we are compared to athletes and competition in the pages of the Bible.

The Apostle Paul likens the life of the believer as to an athlete running a race. I like to tell people that they are not running a sprint; or even a 40 or 100 yard dash. No, our life is more like running a long-distance marathon. It's a long race which will take intestinal fortitude, perseverance, and most of all, an unshakable faith in God's plan for our life. All the while, *expect* the evil one to attack you and your family in order to dissuade, discourage, and detour you from God's perfect plan and purpose for your life. Come what may, keep your eyes fixed upon Jesus Christ.

"Therefore then, since we are surrounded by so great a cloud of witnesses (who have borne testimony to the Truth), let us strip off and throw aside every encumbrance (unnecessary weight) and that sin which so readily (deftly and cleverly) clings to and entangles us, and let us run with patient endurance and steady and active persistence the appointed course of the race that is set before us.

Looking away (from all that will distract) to Jesus, Who is the Leader and Source of our faith (giving the first incentive for our belief) and is also its' Finisher (bringing it to maturity and perfection)" (Hebrews 12:1-2a, Amplified).

Keep your eyes on the prize, and His name is Jesus!

Please allow these words to sink deep within your spirit: The only person who doesn't feel the viciousness and constant bombardment of the spirit, mind and flesh of temptation is the one who has already surrendered to Satan.

The Bible shows that the closer one is to God, the more severely he or she will be tempted.

"This High Priest of ours understands our weaknesses, for he faced all of the same testings we do, yet he did not sin" (Hebrews 4:15, NLT).

Keep in mind that Jesus was also tempted in various ways that we aren't. To know the temptations of Christ, an individual would have to be like Him. The more Christ-like a believer is; the more severe his temptations will be. The more you live in the Light, the brighter and shinier you become as a target for the adversary. Count on it.

What you should be working toward now is to have your life make an *eternal* impact upon the lives of others-no matter where you work or what you do for a living, and God will protect and take care of you. When the wicked one comes knocking on the door to your soul trying to sell you on something really tempting, and too good to be true, just say 'no!' Make a quality decision in your heart today to be a man or woman of integrity and honor. God's Word commands us to "flee from sin." That means: *RUN!* Loved one, *being tempted* is not sin, however, giving in to that desire, and acting upon the temptation *is sin.*

I once heard Dr. Charles Stanley give a vivid illustration on the seductive allure of temptation, and the danger of giving in to sin.

To the best of my memory, I'll paraphrase:

A little child is running around the inside the house and playing on a cold winter's day and spots his Mom building a fire inside the family's fireplace. She's twisting up pages of newspaper and placing kindling wood in between, and on top of the paper. Mom then carefully strikes a match and then she ignites the newsprint. Mommy warns this little guy to keep away at a safe distance as she closes the fireplace screen then proceeds to the kitchen. The little boy, maybe three or four years-old, sees the small fire beginning to burn with different colors shooting upward from the logs. He slowly begins moving closer toward the fire and feels its warmth. "Hey this looks fun." He thinks he could make the blaze even bigger and brighter, and so he opens the protective screen *just a little,* and tosses tissues, one after another, at the fire. What would happen if he poked it with his Mom's broom sitting nearby? Wow! Sparks are now popping and erupting from the blazing wood as the little guy gets more and more excited and perilously closer. An errant spark suddenly explodes from the flames like a burning coal on to the child, igniting his clothing, and he runs through the house in flames, screaming in terror toward his horrified mother.

Dr. Stanley then asked the question at the conclusion of this illustration: "When did the little boy's clothing catch fire?" It would be easy to tell just by looking at a clock. However, from a spiritual standpoint, this boy went up in flames the moment he started *moving toward* the fire.

Dear friend, our loving Savior has promised that He would never leave or forsake His own, even to the end of the age. Call out to the Lord right now, wherever you are and ask Him to forgive your sins, come in to your life as Savior, Lord and Friend, and He will fill you to overflowing with His Spirit and will strengthen and empower you!

"The temptations in your life are no different from what others experience. And God is faithful. He will not allow the temptation to be more than you can stand. When you are tempted, He will show you a way out so that you can endure" (1 Corinthians 10:13, NLT).

Don't put yourself into surroundings or situations that you know are weak spots in your life, but if you fall, fall toward Jesus. If you sin, don't run from Jesus, instead, run to Him! Make every failure a stepping stone to ultimate victory.

"If we confess our sins; He is faithful and just to forgive us our sins, and to cleanse us from all unrighteousness." (1 John 1:9, NKJV)

4

Slip-Sliding Away
(The deadly nature of backsliding)

The term "backslider" or "backsliding" has been used in Christian circles for centuries. It's found in the Bible some seventeen times. Here are some instances where the term is used from the book of Jeremiah:

"*Return O <u>backsliding</u> children,*" *says the Lord; "for I am married to you" (3:14, NKJV).*

"*Because their (Jerusalem's) transgressions are many, their <u>backslidings</u> have increased." (5:6, NKJV)*

"*O Lord, our iniquities Testify against us…for our <u>backslidings</u> are many; we have sinned against you" (14:7).*

Backsliding means; *"turning ones' back on God."* The Bible says that God's people backslid mostly after times of amazing prosperity and blessing. So often, when the Lord poured out loving mercies on His people, they soon turned away from Him. At this point I must clearly state a crucial point: You can *willfully* turn away from God or even be in a "state of drifting" *and not even realize it* until it's tragically, too late.

"*Therefore a lion out of the forest shall slay them, a wolf of the deserts shall destroy them, a leopard will watch over* *their cities. Everyone that goes out from there shall be torn in pieces, because their transgressions are many; their <u>backslidings</u> have increased. How shall I pardon you for this? Your children have forsaken me, and sworn by those that are not gods. When I had fed them to the full, then they committed adultery and assembled themselves by troops in the harlots' houses. They were like well-fed lusty stallions; Every one neighed after his neighbor's wife" (Jeremiah 5:6-8, NKJV).*

In these verses, the Prophet Jeremiah describes in detail just *what* and *who* a backslider is. The backslidden person is one who once enjoyed the blessings and favor of God.

This person was, at one time, a child of God. He or she had a vital and intimate relationship with God. He or she loved to pray and just spend time with the heavenly Father. They had promised God, "Lord, I will always follow and serve you with all of my heart." For a while, this child of God was faithful to his pledge. He had turned away from sin and pursued the things of God with a passion. He loved spending time with God and in the Word. He couldn't wait for the fellowship he found with other believers in the local church. He'd gotten involved wholeheartedly in ministry; being a blessing to other people. However, something began to distract, and slowly draw this child of God away from the Lord. This person's love was no longer white-hot as before…he'd found it was becoming cooler, and then eventually, cold. His love for God was no longer genuine, and soon lost his fear of the Lord. Hypocrisy crept into his life ever so slowly. It started with little things like 'fudging' on his taxes, and in the books at work. He no longer had time for God. No time for fellowship with other believers. He became distracted with other things which drew his attention away from God, and solely onto the things of this world. The main thing was no longer the main thing.

In the end, this backslidden one totally revolted against, and finally, rejected God. He is now blind, devoid of understanding, and what God calls, "a fool," on the fast-track heading toward eternal destruction. The Bible is ever so clear:

God views backsliding as *evil.* Backsliding has terrible and tragic consequences.

"'Your own wickedness will correct you, and your backslidings will rebuke you. Know therefore and see that it is an evil and bitter thing that you have forsaken the Lord your God, and the fear of Me is not in you,' says the Lord of hosts" (Jeremiah 2:19, NKJV).

God is grieved and saying to this wayward one, "How could you have rejected and turned from me, when I blessed, sustained, and loved you as my own child? Yet you turned and walked away."

Listen dear friend, God loves you, but do you really believe that He will just sit back and allow the wicked one to take you hostage from Him? Do you honestly think He will let you turn away and head down the wide road of eternal destruction? Pay careful attention to the words of Jesus when He says; ***"Enter by the narrow gate; for wide is the gate and broad is the way that leads to destruction, and there are many who go in by it. Because narrow is the gate and difficult is the way which leads to life, and there are few who find it" (Matthew 7:13-14, NKJV).***

God will not allow you to sprint headlong into hell without setting numerous roadblocks along the way in order to get your attention before it's too late. There are terrible consequences for the sin of backsliding. May I present to you just a few?

When God finally confronts the backslidden person, it affects everybody within his sphere of influence. When the backslider's storm eventually hits, it directly or indirectly impacts everyone around him; his spouse, children, friends, coworkers, and even complete strangers.

How many times have you heard a drug addict or a porn addict or an alcoholic's protestations of, "Can't you just leave me alone? My addiction is a personal issue! It's my problem alone. I'm not hurting anybody but myself!"

This is patently untrue. As a Pastor, I cannot begin to tell you how many marriages, families, and relationships I have seen decimated *within the Church of Jesus Christ* by what society labels as an "addiction" or a "sickness" (where the person is helpless and bears no personal responsibility for his or her choices) but contrary to our culture, the Bible clearly calls it "bondage." Friend, if you're trapped and in bondage because of the choices you've made; *your* problem has been thrust upon everyone who lives with you, those who work with you, and those that know you. You are becoming dangerous to be around because of what you're exposing everyone else to, whether directly or indirectly. Sadly, the backslider all too often ends up destroying his or her entire family. You'll find that God's Word clearly states that '*no one* lives or dies unto himself.' That means we are all inextricably linked to one another emotionally and spiritually. Though I may con myself into thinking that what I do in my private life has nothing to do with my public position as a husband, father, and minister…The Bible says otherwise.

"Surely I have sinned, and have done wickedly; but these sheep, what have they done? Let your hand, I pray, be against me and against my father's house" (2 Samuel 24:17, NKJV).

"You have sinned against the Lord; and be sure; your sin will find you out" (Numbers 32:23, NKJV).

Loved one, at one time, maybe you were a 'living Epistle' in your workplace or classroom. You were eager and excited to talk with other people about Jesus Christ, and the wonderful things He had done for you and everybody knew something was different about you. But now, all that is in the past. They look at you, and interact with you and realize that something's changed, and not for the better. They see that you're now becoming like one of them. Have you ever stopped to consider that your life and witness may have been someone's last hope? Yes, they probably had poked fun at you behind your back at one time, but in their heart of hearts believed that, "Sure, he was a little strange and a bit of a fanatic, but he was somebody I could approach when I was in trouble or hurting."

Please understand that a backslidden believer presents a distorted, even perverse picture of Christianity to the world because now, your coworkers, family and mere acquaintances will say,

"Why are you so bummed out lately? You've even stopped trying to get me to visit your church. Have you given up on your God?"

If you are running from God, whatever the reason, download this: The farther that you move away from beyond the Lord's hedge of protection; the further in you are treading upon Satan's territory, and know that your crisis is on its way. If you don't change your mind and change direction soon *(that's "repentance")*, realize a storm is on its way, and it will be devastating. A massive storm hitting you now in your weakened spiritual condition, and will bring about the darkest and most critical circumstances in your life.

Are you, as the famous Paul Simon song goes, "slip-sliding away?"

As I study and gain understanding from God's Word on this subject, I believe there are two diametrically opposed options available to anyone who finds themselves in a backslidden condition today.

The first is the less desirable of the two choices. One can give up and give in to a sense of hopelessness, depression and defeat by believing the lie that you're too far gone for God to ever forgive and restore. This mindset will give the adversary the upper hand in your life and sink you, as if in quicksand, deeper into the depths of despair. You may even think God has abandoned you and are thinking, "It's just so futile. Maybe I am lost forever. I must deserve all of this trouble and heartache in my life."

Right now you have a choice to make, my friend. You can give in to hopelessness and be taken prisoner and beaten from pillar to post by the wicked one, or…

You could get up from where you are right now, and cry out to God for mercy. You can come back to Jesus Christ, no matter how far away from Him you've tried to run! Our loving and compassionate Savior is, I believe, even now, wooing your heart, and gently urging you to return to your first love, but you must *choose* to do it wholeheartedly.

"Today, I set before you death and life; blessing and cursing, therefore choose life that you may live."

I love what the prophet Jonah had prayed to God upon repenting with sincere brokenness over his own sin: "I cried out to the Lord because of my affliction, and He answered me. Out of the belly of Sheol (Hell) I cried, and you heard my voice" (Jonah 2:2, NKJV).

Friend, you too can make the right choice when you open your heart and pray: *"When my soul fainted within me, I remembered the Lord; and my prayer went up to you into your holy temple…But I will sacrifice to you with the voice of thanksgiving; I will pay what I have vowed. Salvation is of the Lord" (Jonah 2:7, 9, NKJV).*

If any backslider will simply turn back toward Jesus, our Lord promises to forgive and to restore everything the adversary has taken from you. God will not only restore everything; He will multiply it! We have His Word on it!

"Surely as a wife treacherously departs from her husband, so have you dealt treacherously with Me, O house of Israel," says the Lord…"For they have perverted their way; they have forgotten the Lord their God. Return, you backsliding children, and I will heal your backslidings." Indeed we do come to you, for you are the Lord our God" (Jeremiah 3:20-22, NKJV).

Loved one, all you have to do, is simply, *return.*

5

I Resent That!

Resentment" defined: "When I drink poison, and then wait for you to die"

"My close friends detest me. Those I loved have turned against me" (Job 19:19, NLT).

How do you handle hurt? I'm not talking headaches or hemorrhoids. How do you handle those hurts that inevitably happen in life which cause anger and emotional pain? These are the hurts that can last for years or even a lifetime if left unchecked. Please, never ignore your hurt, because when you ignore it, that hurt grows like a dangerous tumor, and spreads like a cancer in your soul. Its final death-dealing stage metastasizes into hatred.

I think if anybody had an excuse to become bitter and resentful, it might be our boy, Job, from the Old Testament. Job was like the Donald Trump or Bill Gates of his day. He was the wealthiest dude that existed, at that time in history. However, in one day's time, one 24-hour period, this powerful man lost everything. All of his children were tragically killed. Job went bankrupt. His world fell completely apart. You would think he had a right to be bitter. All Job had left that remained was a negative, nagging wife who almost harangued him into the grave. Job also had a few close friends who came by to "bless him." The attitude of his buddies was, "Job, dawg, this is all your fault man! Obviously, you must have brought all this mess on yourself. God's getting you back for something!"

"If my misery could be weighed, and my troubles could be put on the scales, they would outweigh all the sands of the sea." (Job 6:2-3, NLT)

"He will not let me catch my breath, but fills me with bitter sorrows" (Job 9:18, NLT).

Can you identify with any of these sentiments?

There's much to learn here from Job's story. Let's be clear: It's wise for us to learn from experience, but even wiser to learn from the experiences of others.

Job was becoming bitter. He even began to fix the blame on God. He said so himself. His close friends were obviously no help because in amateur attempts to psychoanalyze the situation, they'd said some very hurtful things to Job.

Are you still hurting over some of the terrible things said to you or about you from your past? They may have occurred in the distant past (in your childhood) or fairly recently. Nevertheless, those words have cut you like a knife, and you'll never forget them.

"Thoughtless words wound just as deeply as any sword" (Proverbs 12:18, Amplified).

Rejection is also very painful; especially when you're doing your best, trying to please someone but they reject it in the end. Possibly the rejection came from Daddy, or Mama, or a school teacher. You were told in no uncertain terms that you'd never measure up to an older sibling, or that 'your best just wasn't good enough.' So often, the very people we are trying to please the most are those whom we love the most. It's extremely rare for us to resent a stranger. However, it's the folks we are closest to who have the most profound impact upon our lives. All of this is extraordinarily confusing for a child to process—let alone an adult who's been rejected and hurt. You may have experienced the devastating pain and rejection of a spouse that was unfaithful to you by going out and having an affair with one of your closest friends or relatives. The pain is indescribable.

I must warn you that the Bible says that resentment and its ensuing bitterness can eat you alive. It is unreasonable, foolish, and irrational: It's dumb. Your resentment and bitterness changes nothing. It doesn't make right a wrong. It doesn't solve the problem. It'll surely never restore a relationship. You are not hurting the other person at all. You are hurting *you*. You are actually drinking a tall, cold glass of spiritual poison, and then waiting for the *other guy* to die! You become so consumed with the past that you are in fact, destroying your present. Bitterness is emotional and spiritual attempted suicide.

You are only hurting yourself with your anger (Job 18:4, Amplified).

Spiritual, emotional, and physical health and wellbeing are all connected. Sin, sickness, and disease are often intertwined. Medical science has determined that resentment/bitterness is the single, most *unhealthy* emotion that a human being can have. Just look at some of the conditions that can be directly attributed to it: Headaches, backaches, arthritis, and ulcers: The list goes on and on. God's Word is explicit: ***"Resentment kills" (Job 5:2).*** So how do I eliminate resentment from my own life?

Tell God exactly how you feel. Let off steam and unload. Be brutally honest; cry out to the Lord and yell, if you have to! Job did as did David, and lots of folks in the Bible as well. It's called being human. God created the wide range of emotions inside each one of us. He is a BIG GOD: He can handle your frustration, anger, bitterness, bewilderment, and exasperation!

He's not going to fry you like a slice of bacon when you become authentically; ***honest to God.***

God patiently allowed Job to unload his emotional distress and mess. It was a moment of hot tears, shouting, anger, and frustration for Job. It was an intense personal, cathartic, cleansing experience, and became the turning point of Job's tribulation. Listen to this man, Job, at the absolute end of his rope, honestly encountering the Lord:

"I am weary of my life and I loathe it! I will give free expression to my complaint; I will speak in the bitterness of my soul. I will say to God, Do not condemn me [do not make me guilty]! Show me why You contend with me…Have You not poured me out like milk and curdled me like cheese?...If I am wicked, woe unto me! And if I am righteous, yet must I not lift up my head, for I am filled with disgrace and the sight of affliction…You renew Your witnesses against me and increase Your indignation toward me; I am as if attacked by a troop time after time…Are not my days few? Cease then and let me alone, that I might take a little comfort and cheer up" (Job 10:1, 2, 10, 15, 17, 20, Amplified).

Following Job's rant, what do you think God did? How did He react? Did God get in Job's face and snarl back, "Are you talking to me? Are you talking to me? Oh, yeah, you must be talking to me because ain't nobody else here except you and me!" No, God didn't 'go off' on Job. God was silent. You'd think He'd crush Job like a bug on the sidewalk. However, God is not surprised or shocked by our passion or emotional outbursts. He created those very emotions. The Lord gave you the capacity to get angry and express those feelings. He understands you completely, dear one.

Is any of this beginning to sink in? If so, you're getting ever closer to soaring with eagles, and leaving your "buzzards" behind! Once you begin to get real with God, and yourself, about your emotions and internal pain, you will be ready to move up to the very next step which may be the most difficult of all: Forgiving those who've hurt you.

6

It's My Life

"For if you do not forgive men their trespasses, neither will your heavenly Father forgive your trespasses" (Matthew 6:14-15, NKJV).

You will never stop hurting, or begin to live victoriously until to learn to *forgive:* Totally, utterly and completely forgive. Jesus did just that on the Cross as He cried out, ***"Father, forgive them, for they know not what they do."*** "Well, hold on now," you say, "That was Jesus Christ. I'm nowhere near in the same league as he was. He's God!" You are correct. The Bible says that He was fully God, *and* fully man. No one in all of history suffered and died as He did, for the sin of all humankind, for all time. What makes you think it was any easier for Jesus to forgive than for you to? You and I can obtain His love and power to forgive those who have violated us in one way or another. It's only through the presence and power of Christ, that you can let go, forgive, and release others and in the process, you too, will be free.

Looking back at ole' Job again, we read that his friends did hurt him, but then in Job 42, verse 10, the Bible says, ***"After***

Job prayed for his three friends the Lord made him prosperous again and gave him twice as much as he had before." When did Job's trials, tribulations, and depression come to an end? When he got his revenge on those guys? No way! It was after he forgave his friends…when he prayed for them. He had released them and let them go. He did this even though he was still hurting.

Exactly how can you know for sure when you've truly forgiven, and released that particular individual who's hurt you in your life? You will know for sure when you can pray for their success. You will know when you can pray (continually) for theirs and their family's blessing and wellbeing. When you can do these things; the resentment and bitterness will lift, and leave you, and you'll know you've released them.

Listen to the words of Jesus:

"But I tell you who hear Me, Love your enemies. Do good toward those who hate you. Bless those who mistreat you" ***(Luke 6:27, NKJV).***

In order to forgive, I must be willing to change *my attitude* about a relationship that's on the rocks. Someone once said, *"Forgiveness is the perfume of a crushed flower on the heel of the one who trampled it."*

I also need to lay hold of the fact that forgiveness is not based on my feelings. Forgiveness is a conscious decision that I make. In my years as a Pastor, I have listened to a lot of truly shocking and heartbreaking stories from people that God has put in my spiritual care. I've listened as young women have shook violently, with hot tears, describing in agonizing detail how their father, uncle, or someone they'd trusted, would repeatedly molest them when these women were little girls. I've heard firsthand accounts of substance and domestic abuse; stories of brutality inflicted upon children, as well as sins of adultery, and a myriad of other horrific ways in which people hurt one another.

Possibly you were violated in a very profound way. Maybe your parents caused you harm, or your spouse has rejected you, or someone may have even sabotaged your job or career. Even though you were the victim of another person's sin, you can be healed by the power of forgiveness. Forgiveness is not a feeling: It is a decision. It is a conscious act of your will.

Who do you think benefits the most when you forgive the person who hurt you? Forgiveness isn't necessarily for the one who injured you. Your willingness to forgive them sets you free! You aren't giving in to their meanness or condoning their cruelty toward you. You are not whitewashing the words or actions of your offender. You are forgiving them in order to bring cleansing to you! Forgive, and release, and you will free your mind and heart from the toxic poison of that painful memory.

In Matthew's gospel, chapter 5, verses 23 and 24, Jesus tells us to make forgiveness our immediate priority. Forgiveness must be offered now.

Jesus said, *"Therefore, if you bring your gift to the altar, and there remember that your brother has something against you, leave your gift there before the altar, and go your way. First be reconciled to your brother, and then come, and offer your gift."*

Get up off your knees, and go, be reconciled to your brother: Immediately. Just do it. Make things right between you. Get it done now, *and then* return to your place of prayer. All that other stuff you're doing in the church or for your neighborhood is meaningless until to decide to confront the unforgiveness in your own heart.

Then Peter came up to Him and said, "Lord, how many times may my brother sin against me and I forgive him and let him go? [as many as] up to seven times?" Jesus answered him;"I tell you, not up to seven times, but seventy times seven" (Matthew 18:21-22, Amplified).

What the Lord was saying was, 'Forgive and forgive some more until it becomes habit!' Quit keeping score. Forgive quickly, completely and continually. I want to tell you that uncontrolled anger, bitterness and hatred are terribly costly to the human soul. They could cost your very life; both here and in the world to come. However, forgiveness saves the expense of anger and the high price of hatred which decimates your spiritual, mental, and physical energy.

Need another good reason to forgive? Read on.

"For if you do not forgive men their trespasses, neither will your heavenly Father forgive your trespasses" (Matthew 6:14-15, NKJV).

Friend, you have only two options to choose from: You can change your direction and forgive or stay hard-hearted, unforgiving, and destroy yourself. It's really that cut-and-dry. Your own future is on the line. If you will not forgive others, Almighty God will not forgive you. Someone once said, *"He who will not forgive others, burns the bridge over which he must pass in through the gates of heaven."* That's powerful, and so true. Life is much too short to waste away by holding onto grudges, being petty, carrying bitterness, or eaten alive by hatred that builds up over time. Loved one, make a conscious choice to forgive now from the heart and be *free*.

Do you remember Job? We haven't forgotten about him or his trials and tribulations, but have saved the end of his story for now. God did come to Job's rescue and He also provided a reprimand, encouragement, comfort, and supernatural provision. The Lord blessed Job with a very happy ending.

"Then the Lord blessed the last part of Job's life even more than he had blessed the first" (Job 42:12, NKJV).

Job suffered terribly throughout this story which experts say lasted a period of time between nine to ten months of his life. However, God mercifully delivered Job, and blessed the last part of his life much more than He had the first. The core message of Job's story is this: It makes no difference as to who has injured or violated you, or how long you've carried that hurt. The Lord wants to make the rest of your life the best of your life! You must first be willing to *forgive* every offense, and *release* the offender. In so doing, you will be more like Christ, and you will be set free.

Might you still be holding on to painful memories from your past? Was something said or done to you long ago that may have crushed your self-esteem and spirit? Was something done to you by someone that inflicted pain and emotional devastation which has lingered in your mind and heart for a long time? Maybe it occurred many years ago, but it is still fresh in your memory as if it happened only yesterday. Refusing to deal honestly with your own feelings and withholding forgiveness toward your offender will adversely affect your entire life.

Possibly you will need to make peace with your father or mother for something that's haunted you since childhood. Might you need to forgive an ex-spouse because you've carried around the excess emotional baggage and it's causing serious problems in a current personal relationship(s)? You just might have had your job or career sabotaged by a coworker with no scruples. Don't allow certain people or the pain they have caused to hurt you anymore. It will literally make you sick. For your own sake, forgive them. Release them in your heart. You might be saying to yourself, "I know I should forgive them. The Bible says so, but I just can't."

This is the reason why you need Jesus Christ. Only Christ can give you the inner power to forgive, and He alone can heal your broken heart.

There was a dark period in my own life when, I too, carried around and clutched bitterness with a clenched death-grip, and would not let go. I was an angry child who grew into an angry man. For me, it all began with a broken heart around the age of nine. My mother approached me on a Sunday afternoon, and in emotional anguish, informed me that Daddy was leaving home for good. He had filed for divorce. "Why doesn't he want us anymore? What did I do wrong? It's only going to be Mommy, Sissy and me...forever?"

Almost like "Dr. Jeckyl & Mr. Hyde," my personality changed immediately and radically. I morphed from being quite the Mama's boy and I became more and more aggressive—both verbally and physically.

For the ensuing twenty-plus years, my life was consumed with alcohol and substance abuse. I'd bragged about my so called "rock-n-roll rebel" lifestyle. It was all about sex, drugs and rock-n-roll. I was a mean and out-of-control person. I honestly don't know how I didn't end up dead during those "lost years" although there were a number of close calls.

In February of 1984, I thought I'd hit the jackpot, gotten lucky, and found the woman of my dreams. Her name was Debbie, and she had long flowing brown hair and the most beautiful green eyes (she's Irish don't ye' know). Whoa!!! I was totally smitten, and I also truly believed that she alone would be the one who would save my life; which was completely unfair to her. After we were married on November 3, 1984, reality soon came crashing in on both of us. I began to realize that Debbie wasn't equipped or willing to be my 'savior.' It wasn't very long into our marriage when she had a 'revelation' that she was married to an absolute jerk. Things spiraled downward in our relationship for the several years, and I certainly hadn't changed for the better, until I eventually suffered a nervous breakdown in 1986. My emotional crash could have totaled our entire marriage. As dark and hopeless as things appeared at the time, my emotional implosion became the turning point of my entire life. For the next twelve months I sought professional help. Over time, through the skill and compassion of my counselor; the sometimes "tough love" I received from Debbie, and the unconditional love from my Mom and family, I began to develop a deep curiosity about God that I hadn't had since ages four through eight, when I'd sensed some sort of divine calling on my life. As I became stronger (and saner), I took up another habit which soon replaced the cocaine, killer weed, and the Tennessee bourbon that I couldn't do without, I started watching TBN, the Trinity Broadcasting Network. I must admit that it wasn't with the most noble of intentions. I remember clicking it on just so I could laugh at and crack on "those weird, goofy characters" but I was soon hooked. These people had something I didn't, but I began to really want it. Several weeks after I first began tuning in to TBN, I caught a recorded, on-location "Praise the Lord" program with Paul and Jan Crouch. Candi Staton was on that program singing "Highway to Heaven," and the late, great, Dr. E.V. Hill preached the message which would change my life—for all eternity. Yes, something was very different that afternoon in Dayton, Ohio as I began a new regiment of lifting weights and getting physically fit. My inner man, the spirit, was getting fed and nourished through viewing TBN and a new found curiosity and hunger for the Bible (The Bible of all things!).

It was, as I lay on my weight bench and just about to start bench-presses, when Dr. E. V. Hill caught my attention. To this day, I couldn't tell you the theme of his message, but I do remember his powerful words on man's hopelessness, God's unconditional love, mercy, and grace. He spoke so passionately on how God *wants to* forgive me of all the sin in my life, and make me His own child; from the moment that I receive Jesus Christ into my heart as personal Savior and Lord. I then, physically, felt that some invisible force…no, *someone* was in the room with me. I was not alone. I was at first, overwhelmed, and then began to cry. It wasn't the type of crying I'd become accustomed to; those used to be tears of despair, hopelessness, from deep within my lost soul. However, now, in almost the blinking of an eye, my weeping drastically changed. It was now my soul's response to the warmth of God's tangible presence and amazing love which was now enveloping me on my weight bench.

Pastor Hill on the television then proceeded to invite people to open their hearts and lives, to accept Jesus Christ as personal Savior. I jumped up from the weight bench; my face now covered with tears, and I prayed the simple prayer of salvation with that man of God on the television. Instantly the tears and emotions intensified as I suddenly realized I was now *clean* on the inside. Then I experienced something similar to that of very warm oil, like a "liquid love" being poured upon my head and overflowing throughout my entire being. It felt as if two invisible arms were embracing me *physically.* It was then that I heard in my spirit, these words, *"I've waited a long time to hear you pray those words. Son, because you have given yourself totally to me; I now give myself unto you. Now, child, remember my calling upon your life when you were four. That's never been removed."* My new life began at that moment.

You may be asking the very same questions I asked back then. "Is it really that simple to make Jesus the Lord of my life? Is that what it means to be *born again*?"

Today is the day of salvation. Now is the appointed time. There's a Latin term, *"carpe diem,"* which means; *"seize the day."* Friend, this is your day, and your moment in which your eternal destiny hangs in the balance. Jesus Christ stands in the doorway of your heart right now, and he is knocking. You've tried, but failed miserably living life according to your unofficial theme song, the popular, *"It's My Life."* No it's not. Your life is not your own. It was given to you by God in order to develop a personal, intimate, and loving relationship with Him through Jesus Christ, His Son. It was given to you in order to prepare you for eternity with Him.

Take Job's advice right now, wherever you are, and *"reach out to God!"*

Would you pray with me?

"Dear God, I don't understand exactly what I'm doing, but I know for sure that I want my heart to be right with you, Lord. I've been carrying a load of hurt and have been toting around excess baggage of resentment toward those who've caused me pain. It's made me sick inside, Lord. Please forgive me for my hard heart, and remove this bitterness and resentment out of my life. Replace my pain with God's peace. Replace my anger with your healing power. Exchange my fear with faith; and my bitterness with love. My Lord and my God, at this moment, I choose to forgive _____, and pray for their blessing. Help me to face the world again, and please help me to focus on Jesus as my personal Savior and Lord. I don't know what my future holds, but I now know who it is that holds my future. Heavenly Father, I will live for you and serve you all the days of my life. In Jesus' wonderful name I pray. Amen."

Loved one, your "buzzards" are now scattering.

"The eagle has landed!"

7

Child, You Mind Your Daddy!

Therefore be imitators of God as dear children, and walk in love…" (Ephesians 5:1-2a, NKJV).

"How God anointed and consecrated Jesus of Nazareth with the Holy Spirit with the [Holy] Spirit and with strength and ability and in power; how He went about doing good and in particular, curing all who were harassed and oppressed by [the power of] the devil, for God was with Him" (Acts 10:38, Amplified).

How many believers in Jesus Christ are constantly shouting, running, jumping, rolling on the floor, fasting, crying, begging and passionately singing out for *'more love, more power more of you in my life,'* or they'll sing, *'O Lord, send the power just now and baptize everyone'(?).* However, all too often, after the shouting has subsided, and the music has ended, too many people walk out of the church auditorium just as dried-up, malnourished and defeated as when they first walked in a couple hours earlier. Millions and millions of books, CD's and DVD's on the subjects of the Anointing and Spiritual Authority are sold each year. That's a good thing. I own many of these valuable resource materials on these very themes and have been greatly blessed and encouraged by them. However, more often than I'd like to admit, I have felt empty, desperate, powerless, defeated. I was not soaring with *eagles.* No, I found myself (as a Christian, and a Pastor--for crying out loud!) sinking into a quicksand of negativity. Too often, I'd catch myself squawking, sulking, and slinking around with the *buzzards* in utter defeat. *"Hey Lord, I'm busy doing the work of the ministry that you called me to do. I help people. I'm a pretty good husband and father and I provide for my family. Where are you when I really need You, Lord? Where's the anointing and power of the Holy Spirit that I always could depend upon to minister, and to live in? Why am I feeling so dried up, negative, frustrated, and powerless?"*

Something was wrong with *me*; not with God.

I am hardheaded sometimes and have had to learn some valuable lessons in life--the hard way. I want to share with you the most important lesson that I have ever benefitted from. It was so simple! I said *simple: Not easy.* It is not pain-free; although it has long-term implications, rewards, and blessings.

"Let this same attitude and purpose and [humble] mind be in you which was in Christ Jesus: [Let Him be your example in humility]. Who, although being essentially one with God and in the form of God [possessing the fullness of the attributes which make God, God], did not think this equality with God was a thing to be eagerly grasped or retained, but stripped Himself [of all privileges and rightful dignity], so as to assume the guise of a servant (slave), in that He became like men and was born a human being. And as He appeared in human form, He abased and humbled Himself [still further] and carried His obedience to the extreme of death, even the death of the cross! Therefore [because He stooped so low] God has highly exalted Him and has freely bestowed on Him the name that is above every name, that in (at) the name of Jesus every knee should (must) bow, in heaven and on earth and under the earth, and every tongue [frankly and openly] confess and acknowledge that Jesus Christ

is Lord, to the glory of God the Father" (Philippians 2:5-11, Amplified).

These verses state that Jesus relinquished His heavenly privileges and status in order to take upon Himself, human flesh, and while He was totally man, He was at the same time totally God. Loved one, there is a key here: You might even call it the *ignition key* to the authority and anointing of the Holy Spirit. This was the same *ignition key* that even *Jesus,* the only begotten Son of God used. **Obedience** is the *ignition key* to obtaining, and moving in the authority and anointing of the Holy Spirit. Listen to the Lord's own words; *"I say only what I hear My Father say. I do only what I see My Father do."* Jesus was always obedient to wait upon His Fathers timing. We see that throughout the entirety of the New Testament.

In the garden of Gethsemane (Matthew 26:40-54, Amplified), on that soul-wrenching night before His death on the Cross, Jesus surely could have delivered Himself but He knew it was the Father's will that He go to the Cross, and wait for His deliverance. In that garden, with His disciples all fast asleep, the Lord felt the power of darkness closing in all around Him, and He prayed to the heavenly Father from a heart overflowing with indescribable agony, *"Father, remove this cup (of suffering) from me; yet not my will, but your will be done."*

Obedience is not obedience unless there is *another way* we can do it. Jesus could have helped Himself, by calling legions of angels to come to His aid, but He was obedient to His Father's perfect will.

Be especially mindful that our Lord was obedient within His *heart*, and with His *mouth*. Of Christ, the Suffering Servant, the prophet Isaiah wrote, *"He was oppressed, and treated harshly, yet he never said a word. He was led like a lamb to the slaughter. And like a sheep is silent before the shearers, he did not open his mouth" (Isa. 53:7, NLT).* Until you submit your tongue and lips to the will of God, you will have no hope of living a blessed, victorious life and *soar with eagles.*

"(And) the tongue is a fire. [The tongue is] a world of wickedness set among our members, contaminating and depraving the whole body and setting on fire the wheel of birth (the cycle of man's nature), being itself ignited by hell..." (James 3:6, Amplified).

Now check out this next verse:

"The tongue can bring death or life; those who love to talk will reap the consequences" (Proverbs 18:21, NLT).

Over the past few months I've sensed a stirring deep within my own heart and life; as if the Lord was trying to get something over to me. When I finally did get quiet before Him, these words were whispered into my spirit, *"Do you want to soar 'on eagles' wings?' If you want to live a consistent, victorious life, learn more about the Anointing of the Holy Spirit. I want to teach you about the Anointing.*

Then, the very first scripture I opened my Bible to was Acts 1:8. The Lord spoke these words to His followers just before His ascension into to heaven:

"But you shall receive power (ability, efficiency, and might) when the Holy Spirit has come upon you, and you shall be my witnesses in Jerusalem and all Judea and Samaria and to the ends (the very bounds) of the earth" (Acts 1:8, Amplified).

Here, Jesus speaks of the power and presence of the Holy Spirit for those who *open their hearts* and *receive* this wonderful gift...for those whom the Spirit comes upon. The word translated as "power" in this passage, there is a Greek word; **"dunamis."** This means; *"ability, efficiency, might, mighty works, miracles, and mighty deeds."*

In the gospel of Luke 10:19, Jesus describes one major aspect of the authority and power that He confers upon us; the Church:

"Behold, I give you power over all the power of the enemy."

You and I have the right to act upon this authority and power. We have the right of disposal...disposing of the power to deliver, to help, and to benefit other people, according to God's will and in the name of Jesus (Mark 16:15-20). If you will act upon and use the *ignition key* of God's authority and anointing; that *ignition key* being **obedience**...you will be truly mega-blessed in every area of your life!

"Beloved, I would above all else that you prosper and be in health, even as your soul prospers" (3 John 2, KJV).

I don't know about you but this surely sounds like overwhelming, overflowing, *mega*-blessings, and walking in victory, to me! You see, *a prosperous soul is required in order to live a prosperous life!*

"Think of it this way. If a father dies and leaves an inheritance for his young children, those children are not much better off than slaves until they grow up, even though they actually own everything their father had. They have to obey their guardians until they reach whatever age their father set" (Galatians 4:1-2, NLT).

I remember many years ago, when my mother purchased a 1964 Ford Mustang. What a ride! Yes, even back then in 1975, that vehicle was considered the real deal; a collectors' item. There was, however, one minor complication. I was only fifteen years-old, and as much as I whined, complained, begged and squalled; I did not get to drive it until a.) I became of legal age, b.) I took Drivers Education, and c.) I passed the written exam and driving test. May I say that are many people who are *not* living in obedience before God, and yet they want supernatural power and divine authority. Multitudes of these folks want power, but they are *failing* their tests.

When I was a child, I spoke and thought and reasoned as a child. But when I grew up, I put away childish things (1 Corinthians 13:11, NLT).

Again, I repeat: Obedience is the ignition key to God's power and the anointing, and mega-blessings!

8

Meathead

The weapons of our warfare are not carnal but they are mighty through God; for the pulling down of strongholds" (2 Cor.10:4, KJV).

Experts say that children learn obedience. Obedience does not come naturally. If you have children, you witness firsthand, the three major stages of life's growth process that happens right before your very eyes…

Childhood (Birth to elementary school): The era of late night bottles, crying, diapers, car seats, crawling, playpens, training pants, walking, toys, school, learning responsibility, homework, rewards and punishment.

Adolescence: That awkward period stuck between childhood and adulthood; taking notice of the opposite sex and coming into puberty, Junior & Senior High School, high-drama, skin blemishes, and trying to find ones' own identity.

Adulthood: The season when we truly begin to grasp the responsibilities of life, and meet them intelligently head-on. It's a time when we desire true stability in our lives. There are seasons of planning for the future, paying rent, car payments, serious courtship, pursuing a career, marriage, child-rearing, working hard, trying to maintain a healthy lifestyle, middle-age, grandkids, and the golden years.

By no means is this an exhaustive list of descriptions concerning the various stages of life but only a thumbnail sketch for our purposes here. We can easily and accurately compare these three stages of life with the seasons of spiritual growth and maturity that every follower of Jesus Christ must go through. We realize too, that not every person matures into full adulthood physiologically, emotionally *or* spiritually speaking. Think about it: Children and adolescents (as well as those newly reborn in Christ Jesus, as well as immature believers) tend to want their own way, and they do not behave very nicely if they don't get it (just ask most Pastors!).

The Apostle Paul was confronted with several extremely difficult situations that needed to be confronted and corrected within the Church at Corinth. The Christians in Corinth were, on one hand, a very gifted and enthusiastic bunch; however, on the other hand, they were very immature and weak. In his first letter of instruction to the Corinthian Church he wrote the following:

"And I, brethren, could not speak to you as to spiritual people but as to <u>carnal</u>, as to babes in Christ. I fed you with milk and not solid food; for until now you were not able to receive it, and even now you are still not able; for you are still <u>carnal</u>. For where there are envy, strife, and divisions among you, are you not carnal and behaving like mere men?" (1 Corinthians 3:1-3, NJKV)

What does it mean to be "carnal?" Carnality is taken from the New Testament Greek word; **"sarx,"** which Vine's defines as—Flesh, controlled by animal appetites, and sensual; governed by human nature instead of by the Holy Spirit. *Carnality* carries with it the idea of human weakness.

"For the weapons of our warfare are not carnal but mighty in God for pulling down strongholds" (2 Corinthians 10:4, NKJV).

Paul is indicating that fleshly or human weaponry possesses *no* power to defeat the wicked one. Carnal Christians have a tremendously difficult time waging spiritual warfare. Their rebukes and the sheer volume of their shouting at the devil have no power behind it because their lifestyles have no obedience in them. I'll never forget listening to Kenneth Copeland once when he had an interesting and hilarious take on where the Apostle Paul wrote, ***"...to be carnally minded is death, but to be spiritually minded is life and peace." (KJV)*** Brother Copeland said in this particular sermon that when you order *"Chili con Carne,"* that means, you're asking for "Chili with meat." Thus, should there come a time when you're flailing and failing because of your flesh, and some preacher shocks you by calling you a "meathead," don't get offended. He's not insulting you. He is being completely scriptural. He means you are, in fact, being carnally *(meat)* minded *(headed)!* He said, "Then, just repent (turn from sin), and obey God!"

Ephesians chapter 6, verses 1-11 shows that we absolutely cannot put on the full armor of God without an obedient lifestyle to back it up.

Children, obey your parents because you belong to the Lord, for this is the right thing to do. "Honor your father and mother." This is the first of the Ten Commandments that ends with a promise. And this is the promise: If you honor your father and mother, "you will live a long life, full of blessing."

And now a word to you fathers. Don't make your children angry by the way you treat them. Rather, bring them up with the discipline and instruction approved by the Lord.

Slaves, obey your earthly masters with deep respect and fear. Serve them sincerely as you would serve Christ. Work hard, but not just to please your masters when they are watching. As slaves of Christ, do the will of God with all your heart. Work with enthusiasm, as though you were working for the Lord rather than for people. Remember that the Lord will reward each one of us for the good we do, whether we are slaves or free.

And in the same way, you masters must treat your servants' right. Don't threaten them; remember, you both have the same Master in heaven, and He has no favorites.

A final word: Be strong in the Lord's mighty power. Put on all of God's armor so that you will be able to stand firm against all strategies and tricks of the Devil (Ephesians 6:1-11, Amplified).

All believers start out being "carnal," but we must grow up spiritually, just as we do physiologically and emotionally. In the New Testament Greek, the word for "grow" means *to increase*, whether carnally or spiritually: It's the effect of the work of God in our lives. Realize that nothing grows without God. Only the Lord can make something grow or give increase to, and He does just that when we meet His requirements for growth.

You and I will not grow physically if we do not eat right, exercise, and get proper rest. Likewise, we will not grow spiritually if we do not *feed* our spirit-man *on God's Word*, as well as *exercising our faith in His name*, and *resting in Him*. This is God's spiritual fitness program, and when you enroll, it lasts for a lifetime! It will take your total commitment and obedience. It's a lifelong program of learning and submitting; because if we desire to grow up and mature in the things of God, we must *leave our childish ways*, and *begin to obey authority* in our lives.

If you truly desire to soar with the eagles, you must grow up spiritually. You and I know that children do not want any responsibility: They want only the blessings, the goodies, and the fun.

Spiritual growth means that we begin getting involved with people in an area of ministry, and also start taking responsibility for our actions; understanding God's principle…that we will reap what we have sown.

He (Jesus) is the one who gave these gifts to the church; the apostles, the prophets, the evangelists, and the pastors and teachers.

Their responsibility is to equip God's people to do his work and build up the church, the body of Christ, until we come to such unity in our faith and knowledge of God's Son that we will be mature and full grown in the Lord, measuring up to the full stature of Christ.

Then we will no longer be like children, forever changing our minds about what we believe because someone has told us something different or because someone has cleverly lied to us and made the lie sound like the truth. Instead, we will hold to the truth in love, becoming more and more in every way like Christ, who is the head of his body, the church (Ephesians 4:11-15, Amplified).

Grow up into the Head, which is Jesus Christ, and become an *active* part of his body: the Church, if you want to soar on eagles wings!

Jesus wants us to know our authority, and walk in His power; in a full anointing of the Spirit; but we must also know and honor Him, as our universal and supreme Head.

"I pray that you will begin to understand the incredible greatness of his power for us who believe in him. This is the same mighty power that raised Christ from the dead and seated him in the place of honor at God's right hand in the heavenly realms.

Now he is far above any ruler or authority or power or leader or anything else in this world or in the world to come. And God has put all things under the authority of Christ, and he gave him this authority for the benefit of the church. And the church is his body; it is filled by Christ, who fills everything everywhere with his presence" (Ephesians 1:19-22, Amplified).

Jesus Christ is the Head of *all* things and in *every* aspect of our lives. To genuinely grow and mature in Christ, literally means; that one by one, we let go of the little areas that we've always insisted on controlling in our lives, but in which we tend to fail miserably--and we now submit them fully to Him.

Dear friend, as we come to a close, I hope that something that I've said within the pages of this little book was helpful and a blessing to you. Before I share a little prayer with you, I want to leave you with a few reminders of just who you are in Christ Jesus, and review some of the great and precious promises God has freely given you.

Believe that the power and presence of God resides inside you. Ephesians 3:20 tells you that God is able to do exceedingly abundantly above all you can ask or think or imagine in your wildest dreams—according to the power that's at work *in* you.

Believe and lay hold of the truth in 2 Timothy 1:7, that God has not given you a spirit of fear, but power, love, and a sound mind. If you've made Jesus the Lord of your life, this already accomplished!

Cooperate with God by asking for anything and everything you need that pertains to life and godliness. Dream big! You limit God when you do not dream big and ask big.

Do not limit God! You and I limit the Lord when we forget all that He's done for us in the past. We limit Him when we are no longer thankful. Psalm 103 says, *"Forget not all His benefits."*

Expect the heavenly Father to answer your prayers! Never take for granted the power of expectation; believe you receive it before it manifests in your life. Expect the Lord to strengthen and empower you daily with His Spirit. Again, you will limit what God can do in your life when you lower your expectations.

Be filled with the Holy Spirit. Jesus said, *"You shall receive power when the Holy Spirit comes upon you" (Acts 1:8).* Thank God for the Holy Spirit who is already in you upon accepting Jesus Christ as your personal Savior. The Bible says, *"The very same Spirit that raised Jesus from the dead lives in you" (Romans 8:11).*

Be all that you can be in Christ! You've been given the divine power to love as He loves; the power to forgive even as He's forgiven you; the power to heal; the power to speak God's Word and get results (Mark 11:22-26; 16:15-18; Job 22:28)!

9

All of Me

"I beseech you therefore, brethren, by the mercies of God, that you present your bodies a living sacrifice, holy, acceptable to God, which is your reasonable service" (Romans 12:1, NKJV).

Father God is not seeking some halfhearted, fleshly sacrifice from you to simultaneously to placate Him, and salve your conscience. King Saul had attempted to do this and justify himself before the Lord even though Saul had fallen away from God and had opened his soul to evil spirits. Samuel, however, read Saul his mail in this sharp rebuke:

"Has the Lord as great delight in burnt offerings and sacrifices, as in obeying the Lord? Behold, to obey is better than sacrifice, and to heed than the fat of rams. For rebellion is as the sin of witchcraft and, and stubbornness is as iniquity and idolatry. Because you have rejected the word of the Lord, He also has rejected you from being king" (1 Samuel 15:22-23, NKJV).

Those people who do love God, but are *fleshly* and serving their animal appetites, always give halfheartedly. They offer God cheap sacrifices rather than wholehearted obedience.

They'll give the Lord what costs them little to nothing while clutching tightly onto enough to satisfy their own flesh and personal comfort level.

Loved one, I must tell you right now; and you need to be aware that serving God is very costly, but it always pays tremendous dividends. Even in the natural world, we always make investments before the dividends can come back to us. You must give up something in order to get something. Again, this is the spiritual law of sowing and reaping, and you are living according to this principle every single day, whether or not you are a Christian. Sowing and reaping is a spiritual law that's found throughout the entirety of God's Word.

Long, long ago, as Moses led the children of Israel toward the Promised Land, God told His people to "Go up and possess the land!" And what did the people do? They rebelled. They disobeyed God because of the negative and fearful report brought back by 10 of the 12 spies they'd sent to spy out the land. They believed the majority report that said there are fearsome giants (massive dudes) in the land that could squash us like bugs! "We'd better just forget this whole crazy plan and keep our distance!" God called that report, "evil." Only two of the spies, Joshua and Caleb, obeyed and believed God. They'd said, "We are *well able* to take the land!" As the result of their complete obedience to the Lord, Joshua and Caleb were the only two of that *entire generation* of people to enter into the Promised Land!

Dear friend, all of us, at one time or another; stumble blindly through the wilderness of our own selfishness and disobedience, trying to make it on our own to the Promised Land. We also come to those hard spots in life where God says, "Do this" or "That's dangerous; don't do that" or "Let go of this" or "Submit this area to me." When those pivotal moments come, we have some serious decisions to make. The Israelites made some very poor decisions. They walked in their flesh and were very childish while Joshua and Caleb wholeheartedly and completely obeyed God. Those two *sowed obedience* and *reaped great blessings!*

Today, we are living in Christ's New Covenant with even greater blessings than the Old! Now, God requires that we offer our *entire life* and everything we are and everything we will ever be to Him, as a 'living sacrifice.'

"I appeal to you therefore; brethren, and beg of you in view of [all] the mercies of God, to make a decisive dedication of your bodies [presenting all your members and faculties] as a living sacrifice, holy [devoted, consecrated] and well pleasing to God, which is your reasonable (rational, intelligent) service and spiritual worship" (Romans 12:1, Amplified).

In several passages of the Bible, the Lord refers to Himself as "a jealous God," and He will not be satisfied with just 'a small slice' of you. We cannot say, "OK, Lord, let's make a deal. I'll toss you an offering once in a while, but I really can't afford to tithe. How about blessing me anyway?" Or "I'll tithe and give you ten percent of my income, but I'm just not able to give you control of my tongue or my thought life."

Almost two decades ago, God called me again into fulltime ministry. He wanted me to leave a secure job with good pay behind. I also had a wife, two very little children, a mortgage, insurance, and car payments to make. I can tell you today that because my wife and I obeyed the voice of the Lord, we have been greatly blessed in so many areas of everyday life and ministry.

All humankind is in a fallen state due to our natural tendency and inclination toward pride and rebellion against God. Because we are all born into this fallen condition; we will all die. *You will die, and you need to be ready to meet God.* How do you do that? How can one be ready to meet God face-to-face? That is the very reason Jesus Christ came to this earth. He came to die on a Cross for your sin and mine, and when He died on that cross, He said, ***"My God, my God, why have you forsaken me?" (Mark 15:34, NKJV)*** At that moment, God had laid upon Jesus the sins of all of us; your sins, my sins, everyone's sins. We are forgiven by God because of what Jesus accomplished for us on Calvary's Cross. However, He didn't stay on that Cross. He was laid in a tomb, and three days later, He rose again. God raised Him from the dead and today, He is alive! Jesus said, ***"I am the way, and the truth, and the life. No one comes to the Father except through me." (John 14:6, NKJV)*** The only way to God the Father, and then into heaven is through Jesus Christ, for only he died and arose again to take away our sins. Did you know that Buddha reportedly had said at his life's end, "I am still searching for the truth." Jesus said, ***I am the truth…I am the life."*** He could say it because He was God manifest in the flesh, and the proof is in his resurrection from the dead.

Some of you might be looking for peace and satisfaction through drugs and booze. You won't find it there. You've already witnessed that in other people's lives. They're ruined…wasted. We hear and read a lot about binge drinking in our world today. You might have a good time for a couple of hours, but then it all comes crashing down upon you.

Lots more people are searching for pleasure, satisfaction, and even love, through sex. You won't find it there either. Oh yeah, there is pleasure in illicit sex. Sex is a gift given to us from God, and there is no sin in sex--as long as you play by God's rules: One man and one woman; committed in marriage for life. You will not find the meaning of life in illicit sex or in pornography. There's only heartbreak, emptiness and loneliness after it's all over.

If you are hurting today, feeling the pain of abandonment and rejection, I want you to know that **our Heavenly Father has not abandoned you,** and **He never will.** One young person wrote to a minister after she accepted the free gift of eternal life through Jesus Christ and said, "My entire life had been building up to that one moment in time when I finally ran out of myself, and I asked Jesus Christ to take me over."

Shall we agree together in prayer?

Father God, I thank you for loving me and for sending Jesus Christ, your Son, to die for all my sin; past, present and future. By faith, I receive Him as my personal Lord and Savior today. Come and live in my heart, Lord Jesus. Take control of my life. Thank you for making me the righteousness of God in Christ. Help me to live a godly life before my family, friends, and coworkers. I will be a loving person; sensitive, and compassionate toward others. If I do something wrong or hurtful to another, I'll be quick to repent. I will live a Holy Spirit controlled life. Lord, I will be obedient, consistent and faithful unto your calling upon my life. I will walk in love at all times. I will encourage and bless those who ask for my help. Show me how to soar on eagles' wings, O God. Teach me daily how to live a victorious life in Christ Jesus. Help me Lord, to learn and recognize the voice and leading of the Holy Spirit. I wait upon you, Lord. I expect, hope for and in my God. I shall change and renew my strength and power. I shall lift up my wings and mount up to the sun. I am determined to run and not be weary. I shall walk and not faint or become tired. Your favor and grace are as a crown upon my life and I pray that goodness and mercy shall follow me all the days of my life.

In Jesus' wonderful name, I pray. Amen.

Go with God, loved one, and fly like an eagle!

Additional resource materials by Pastor Anthony Sluzas may be requested through Fresh Harvest Church (Assemblies of God) via U.S. Mail, phone or our website

Anthony Sluzas Ministries:
"Bringing God's Love to Broken Hearts, Broken Relationships & Broken Lives"
275 Canyon Road
Morgantown, WV 26508
(304) 594-3717

www.AnthonySluzas.com
www.FreshHarvest-wv.com

www.ingramcontent.com/pod-product-compliance
Lightning Source LLC
Chambersburg PA
CBHW041609220426
43667CB00001B/17